Spiritual Carbon Monoxide: #1 Killer in the Church

By

Minister Joyce A. Nash

CONTENTS

ACKNOWLEDGEMENTS

First and foremost, I give God the glory for blessing me to finish this book because of the obstacles I had to overcome. I give Him the Glory for His Grace to believe in myself and for that, Father, I say thank you.

I want to thank my sister, Brenda Chandler-Johnson, who believe the God in me and is willing to read everything I write, and is bold and kind enough to correct me.

I want to thank my parents for their support, especially my mom for sticking with me and Hadassah Ministries.

I want to thank Pastor Herman Tolar, for much teaching and training, especially in the area of order, thank you sir.

Last, but not least, I give honor to Evangelist Margiree Brown for God using her in many pivotal times in my life.

INTRODUCTION

Carbon Monoxide is a colorless, odorless and tasteless highly toxic poisonous gas. We hear about carbon monoxide during the winter season more than any other time of the year. If it goes undetected, high potency of the gas can slowly attack our nervous systems and hearts without any notice and cause sudden death.

Carbon monoxide detectors can be purchased for our homes, but how do we detect poisonous gasses in our churches?

What detectors do we have to alert us when there is poison seeping inside of us? The detector we have is the Word of God which guides us into all truth. **St. John 16:13.**

Because we have an enemy that wants us to be deceived and it is God's will that we don't.

1
UNBELIEF

¹"Moreover, brethren, I would not that ye should be ignorant, how that all our fathers were under the cloud and all passed through the sea:

²And were all baptized unto Moses in the cloud and in the sea:

³And all did eat the same spiritual meat:

⁴And did all drink the same spiritual drink: for they drank of that spiritual Rock that followed them: and that Rock was Christ.

⁵But with many of them God was not well pleased: for they were overthrown in the wilderness." **1st Corinthians 10:1-5.**

The children of Israel had the greatest thing going on in their lives, Jehovah – the Eternal, Immutable God, was visiting them and His purpose was to deliver them from the hard bondage of Pharaoh's slavery. ***Genesis 15:13-14, Exodus 3:19-22***

He was leading them into a land He had promised their forefathers. A land flowing with milk and honey, already prepared for possession. ***Exodus 3:8***

But the Word of God declared that with many of them, God was not well pleased because they were, *"overthrown in the wilderness." 1ˢᵗ Corinthians 10:5*

Millions did not make it into the promise land because of one thing: **unbelief.**

How could they have not believed God? Many would ask and declare they would have, but would you?

As I was seeking the Lord, I asked Him what made them struggle so much with Him.

I believe He revealed to me that it was the bondages in their minds.

Exodus 1:13-14 declares, [13]*"And the Egyptians made the children of Israel serve with rigour: [14]And they made their lives bitter with hard bondage, in mortar, and in brick, and in all manner of service in the field: all their service, wherein they made serve, was with rigour."*

The Hebrew word for rigour is "Perek" which means to break apart.

The Egyptians' oppression towards the children of Israel broke them and made their lives bitter.

The bitterness in their hearts, made it hard for them to believe God.

Have you ever been broken? Have you ever felt the inside of you becoming stagnant and to a full stop? You don't understand what is going on with you. You begin a project, but can't finish it. You are up one day and down the next. You boldly declare that God is able and then turn around and wonder if He is really for you. You begin to experience mood swings and ungodly attitudes and even multiple personalities start to develop. It could be labeled as "spiritual bi-polar".

Spiritual bi-polar happens when a person has difficulty living in the Kingdom regardless of how much Word is going forth.

Finding stability is fruitless because of the brokenness in your life. You can't rise up and move forward, no matter how hard you try.

Brokenness means *"to be forcibly separated into two or more pieces"* and many of us have experienced being broken and separated into many pieces.

The children of Israel were not only suffering from oppression from the outside, but depression on the inside.

'Oppression' in the Hebrew means *"to be distressed, crushed, to be forced."* The pressure and force is designed to deny you of your being.

Oppression will deny you of your identity in whom God created you to be and force you to become someone or something else. It attacks you from the outside to stop you from living on the inside.

Heaviness used in **Isaiah 61:3** means, ***"somewhat dark, darkish, wax dim."*** Depression can be known as heaviness.

When a person is depressed, there is darkness around them and their life begins to wax dim.

One of the meanings of heaviness *'is to be weighed down or burdened'*. Depression works by pressing your spirit down on the inside of you. It works well with oppression because together they will bring your life to a standstill.

Those of us who have experienced depression know it weakens us to the point of wanting to give up. Where there used to be a flame burning on the inside has now become a flicker, ready to be blown out in a matter of time.

It messes with your vision both naturally and spiritually. Naturally you feel gloom and doom and life never looks good. It robs you spiritually because your vision has become dim and you can't see what God sees.

You believe everything negative and nothing positive. Nothing is right and nothing can go right.

The children of Israel had wrong mindsets and issues before God came on the scene and so did we.

Murmuring and complaining had already set in. Have you ever been around someone that complained all the time? If you can dig at the root, you will find that they were broken somewhere in life, and bitterness and discontentment has set inside their soul.

I must admit that I looked at God regarding the children of Israel, because He knew what He was getting. Sounds familiar? God knew what He was getting before He saved us.

God also knew while demonstrating His great power in Egypt that perhaps they could believe He was able to bring them out of anything including the bondages that was in their hearts and minds.

So it was then, so it is now. God can bring us out of the bondages that have set in us, if we believe Him.

Upon salvation, God brought us into the Kingdom of His Dear Son, but He also knew our minds had to be renewed by the Word of God in order for us to really experience the freedom that is given to us through Christ Jesus. *Colossians 1:13, Romans 12:1, 2*

The Israelites were delivered from Egypt physically, but remained in captivity mentally and their journey became unfruitful. No matter what God did, every encounter they had was doubt instead of faith.

The same temptation is prevalent today and we must take heed to the fact that we are not above the children of Israel.

If we want to be partakers of the promises of God, we must take heed of the warning declared in **Hebrews 3:15-19,** [15]*"While it is said, Today if you will hear His voice, harden not your hearts, as in the provocation.*

[16]*For some, when they had heard, did provoke: howbeit not all that came of Egypt by Moses.*

[17]*But with whom was He grieved forty years? Was it not with <u>them that had sinned,</u> whose carcasses fell in the wilderness?*

[18]And to whom <u>sware He that</u> they <u>should not enter</u> into His rest, but to them that believed not? So we see that they could not enter in because of <u>unbelief.</u>"

If we are not careful, we also will not obtain the blessings and promises given unto us through Christ Jesus because of one thing: **<u>Unbelief.</u>**

2

LACK OF KNOWLEDGE

"My people are destroyed for lack of knowledge: because thou hast rejected knowledge, I will also reject thee, that thou shalt be no priest to me: seeing thou have forgotten the law of thy God, I will also forget their children." **Hosea 4:6**

This passage of scripture is so powerful that we often quote the *"a"* part of it and don't realize that all affects our relationship with God and our children.

'My People', when God speaks of 'my people', He is speaking of those who are in covenant with Him.

'Are destroyed for a lack of knowledge', to be destroyed in the Greek means *"to be dumb or silent, to fail or perish, to destroy, cease, be brought to silence, and be undone."*

What a victory it would be for the enemy to silence the people of God! How else can he do it except we be in ignorance?

It is God's will for us to have knowledge of Him in every area of our lives. The enemy fights hard against that because he knows once we receive revelation knowledge and truth; we have the opportunity to be delivered from the state of ignorance that has plagued many of our lives.

'Because thou has rejected knowledge.' Do we have an understanding how we can reject knowledge? This happens when we read the Word of God and we won't believe it. When we hear God's voice through vessels that He has chosen to use and we won't receive it.

We must receive the Word of God with meekness in order not to falter because of ignorance. *James 1:21, 1st Peter 2:2*

'I will reject thee.' If only we could hear the testimonials of Cain, King Saul, the kings of Judah and Israel!

Cain would say, "If I only had submitted of what was asked of me", King Saul would say, "Cain, I wished I had submitted and obeyed." King Rehoboam would say, **"**I could have sat on the throne of my grandfather David until all my days were fulfilled, if I would had followed in his ways and served God like I was commanded."

For the Word of the Lord declared that king Rehoboam did evil, because he prepared not his heart to seek the Lord. **2ⁿᵈ Chronicles 12:14**

How many people in churches have been rejected by God for not preparing their hearts to seek Him and have strayed from the Truth into error?

God even proved Himself to King Nebuchadnezzar, a king who was not in covenant with Him, but became a believer of God's Sovereignty, after God allowed him to lose his mind and drove him out of his kingdom for seven years. **Daniel 4:1-37.**

Yet, his grandson, Belshazzar, did not adhere to what his grandfather experienced and disrespected the things of God and God rejected him in the 5th chapter of Daniel.

Will God reject a born again believer?

Read the words of king David unto Solomon; ***"And thou, Solomon my son, know thou the God of thy father, and serve Him with a perfect heart and with a willing mind: for the Lord searched all hearts, and understand all the imaginations of the thoughts: if thou seek Him, He will be found of thee; but if thou forsake Him, He will cast thee off forever."*** **2ⁿᵈ Chronicles 28:9.**

David was letting Solomon know regardless of him being chosen to be king, if he turned away from following God, he would be rejected. Solomon's worship of false idols and disobedience to God's law cost him his throne. God is no respecter of persons.

"That thou should be no priest to me." God held priest at a higher accountability because they had the law. They were to abide by the law and teach the people, being a standard themselves.

God holds men and women that are speaking the oracles of Him to a higher accountability.

While God was speaking to me about being a minister, He took me through some of the passages of the book of Leviticus. I wasn't interested in reading it because in my mind I wasn't doing any sacrifices. Yet, He revealed to me the office of the priest and that it was holy and how I was to live a life according to what was being revealed.

Men and women that are called to speak the oracles of God are accountable to study the Word of God. To always to keep the knowledge of God in their hearts and on their lips because we are God's messengers. **Malachi 2:7**, which declares, *"For the priest lips should keep knowledge, and they should seek the law at his mouth: for he is the messenger of the Lord of hosts."*

God commands those who are called to preach and teach the gospel to be knowledgeable of His Word.

Eli was rejected for having the truth, because he put his sons above the sacred things of God. **1ˢᵗ Samuel 2:27-33**

Hear this next powerful line of scripture, **"Seeing thou has forgotten the law of thy God, I will also forget thy children."**

Our children and children's, children are set to receive the promises of God, but they must be taught the Word of God and see living examples before them.

Deuteronomy 11:18-21 commands:

- *Keep my commandments, (parents, and leaders).*
- *Do the Word by being an example.*
- *Teach your children*
- *Be an example of God before your children and they will prosper and multiply because of seeing your obedience.*

Do you see the transferring of blessings and posterity from God to our children *when we do what we teach?* It is called being an example.

Judges 2:10-11 declares, [10]*"And also all that generation (speaking of Joshua's generation) were gathered unto their fathers: and there arose another generation after them, which knew not the Lord, nor yet the works which he had done for Israel.*

[11]*And the children of Israel did evil in the sight of the Lord, and served Balaam."*

My question unto God was how was it that nothing was made known to that generation about the God of their fathers? About all the wonders He performed in Egypt? What happened?

After reading Joshua the 23rd and 24th chapter, this is what I believe God revealed unto me.

Joshua gathered the children of Israel together, but he called for the leadership first. He called for the elders, heads (over houses and tribes), judges and officers. He rehearsed in their ears the events that had transpired from Abraham to Moses that have led them to this promise land.

He kept referring to the "strange gods" being among them. Joshua made them take another covenant vow to serve God, but he told them to put away the "strange gods" from among them. **Joshua 24:14-15, 19-20, 23-25**

They called themselves <u>serving</u> God as they were <u>worshipping</u> false gods. Jesus said that no man could serve two masters that you would love one and hate the other. **Matthew 6:24**

How could they teach their children about God, when they were unfaithful themselves?

We teach our children what we are. If I am not fully serving God, they will not either. If I am church only, (a pretense of serving God), then they will be church only also. If I am cold and indifferent to the things of God, they will be also.

If I love the Lord and my lifestyle away from the church building exemplifies it before my children, they will learn to have fervency for God, too. It is who we are and what we do that passes down to our children.

The leadership in Joshua's time did not exemplify a true life of living for God before their children, because they never served Him from their hearts.

They were commanded to rehearse the accounts of the God of their fathers and how He delivered them with a great and mighty hand. It was to be rehearsed from generation to generation for them to 1) believe and serve God and 2) possess the promises and blessings He had for them.

Instead of passing down these accounts, the acts and wonders of God was not being mentioned and the children of Israel served false gods the majority of their lives and eventually they went into captivity.

3.

THE SPIRIT OF UNFORGIVENESS

I could not find the word **"Unforgiveness"** itself in my concordance, even though we as Christians have experienced it one way or another.

Whenever there is an altar call regarding **"Unforgiveness"**, we often hear "deliverance from a spirit of Unforgiveness." It is a spirit and it needs an avenue to come through and that is offense.

Having an understanding of how **"offense"** originated will give us better insight why Satan wants us to be ignorant of this **"spirit."**

Offense started with Satan himself who is totally offended with God. He was cast out of heaven and no longer has access to the position, authority, power and relationship he once had with God and on earth.

Ezekiel 28:13-15 declares, *[13]"Thou has been in Eden the garden of God; every precious stone was they covering, the sardius, topaz, and the diamond, the beryl, the onyx, and the jasper, the sapphire, the emerald, and the carbuncle, and gold: the workmanship of the tabrets and of thy pipes was prepared in thee in the day that thou was created.*

[14]Thou art the anointed cherub that covereth; and I have set thee so: thou wast upon the holy mountain of God; thou walked up and down in the midst of stones of fire. [15]Thou wast perfect in thy ways from the day that thou wast created, till iniquity was found in thee."

Look how Satan was created and his position before he fell. His was Lucifer, "son of the morning." Look how beautiful God created him, covering him with precious stones that we spend hundreds of dollars to have. He had pipes and tabrets (musical instruments) for sweet sounds of praise to go forth unto God. He was anointed above all other cherubs.

The position he had was one of authority and power. He had access to the mountain of God, where God Presence dwelled and walked in places with God that is far above our understanding.

When God created him, he was perfect in his ways, being submitted to the will and purpose of God, until iniquity was found in him. **Ezekiel 28:15 declares"** *Thou wast perfect in thy ways from the day that thou wast created, till iniquity was found in thee."*

He was perfect in his ways because of his submission, obedience and worship unto God, but pride set in his heart because of his beauty, because of his position because of his power and authority. Yet he forgot one thing; **he was created!**

No longer did he submit to God's purpose, but to his own. He thought that he could be equal with God, overtake God's authority and sit on God's throne.

Note: anything that has been created can be destroyed.

God dealt with him by casting him out of Heaven.

Isaiah 14:12-15 declares, *[12]"How art thou fallen from heaven, O Lucifer, son of the morning! How art thou cut down to the ground, which didst weaken the nations!*

[13] For thou has said in thine heart, I will ascend into heaven, I will exalt my throne above the stars of God: I will sit also upon the mount of the congregation, in the sides of the north: [14] I will ascend above the heights of the clouds; I will be like Most High.

[15]Yet thou shalt be brought down to hell, to the sides of the pit."

Since the time of Satan's fall and unto now he has a vengeance against God and everything that pertains to Him and that includes us.

God created mankind in His own image and likeness and gave him authority, dominion and power over the earth and Satan. **Genesis 1:26-28, Luke 10:18, 19.**

He needed a way to come against God and he found it in Adam's disobedience it opened up a door to him to execute vengeance mankind.

With sin falling upon mankind, Satan knew it would bring separation from God, but God being all knowing (for he was ahead of him) put in effect the plan of Salvation through His Son, for man sins to be forgiven and restored back to God. **Genesis 3:14-15, 2nd Corinthians 5:19.**

Satan is offended with God and he wants God to be offended with His creation and His creation to be offended with Him. His main objective is to have God's creation rebel against Him, so our fate will be like his: to be cast into the Lake of Fire forever. **Revelation 20:10, 21:18**

He's using the same tactics he used in the Garden of Eden: lies, slander and accusation. He persuaded Adam and Eve to doubt God and his objective is for us to do the same, because Satan doesn't want us to experience God's greatness like he once did.

Not only does he want us to be offended with God, but with each other.

On one hand, he wants us to focus on the circumstances and start speaking contrary to what God is saying, which opens a door to him to bring slander and accusation against God and the other hand, he wants us to focus on each other with our imperfections and slander and accuse one another.

Do you see his subtlety? Our fight is against him, but _we_ have a tendency to accept what _he_ does and _we_ bring his plans to pass, because as I stated earlier, He needs an avenue.

17

Jesus told us in **St. Matthew 18:7** that offense will come and that is because of the sin that is in the world. Everyone that is born into the world has a sin nature and with that comes faults, mistakes, imperfection.

But when we accept Christ as our Savior, the power of God breaks the power of Satan's influence over us and we become a **<u>new</u>** creation in God. **Romans 6:6, 2nd Corinthians 5:17**

Satan's influence is broken to control us to sin and he can't use us at his will, but that doesn't mean we don't still have imperfections and faults.

We must now learn how to walk in this Kingdom through the Word of God and as we start to mature in the Word, we will handle things differently regarding one another.

Can offense be dismantled? Yes, through obeying the Word of God.

St. Matthew 18:15 declares, *"Moreover if thy brother shall trespass against thee, go and tell him his fault between thee and him alone: if he shall hear thee, thou hast gained thy brother."*

Somehow, we have learned how to wear unforgiveness like a **"badge"** and not obey the Word of God in going to the offender. Can I get a witness? Amen.

If unforgiveness cannot be "dismantled" between you and another person, then and only then should a third be included. **St. Matthew 18:15, 16, declares,** *"Moreover if thy brother shall trespass against thee, go and tell him his fault between thee and him alone: if he shall hear thee, thou hast gained thy brother. But if he will not hear thee, then take with thee one or two more, that in the mouth of two or three witnesses every word may be established."*

When we go to someone other than the trespasser, it gives Satan strength to plant a seed and strengthen roots to spread and bring other family members into discord.

Gossip, slander, accusation and the twins, jealousy and envy, anger, resentment and the other extended family members, strife, bitterness, hatred, lying, deception and fault-finding and etc.

Offense is usually a misunderstanding, miscommunication or non-communication about an issue that just needs to be worked out.

I would have to be fair and point out that sometimes offenses come because we won't obey the Holy Spirit when He deals with us about our error and won't go to that person and repent as He leads. The majority of time offense is operating because of our disobedience and pride.

Now, on the other hand sometimes a person doesn't know that they have offended you, so be man or woman enough to tell them and give them a chance to repent.

Stop trying to shout it out, pray it out and give it out and do what Jesus said, leave your gift at the altar and straightened it out and then go shout and dance! **Matthew 5:23, 24**

One thing God has taught me and that is to make sure the offense I am experiencing is real or is it a personal issue going on in the inside of me. If it is personal issue, I have no right to approach them.

Most of us are dealing with emotional childhood issues, marital and low self-esteem issues. No one is to blame for those things that need to be delivered out of your life and demanding someone to fix it is unfair. It is something that needs to be delivered out of you!

Unforgiveness is a major setback in the church and in our personal lives. It blocks God from blessing us, because of His forgiveness of our sins, mistakes and idiosyncrasies.

Why is God commanding us to deal with this and quickly? Because we are giving the enemy what he wants, which is time. Each time we delay obeying God, we give the adversary time to hinder God's will and purpose in our lives, time to block God's blessings for us and time to destroy each other. We just don't have that kind of time!

You and I must make a conscience decision to deal with offense and most of all obey God regarding in this area to keep the enemy dismantled!

4

UNCONFESSSED AND UNREPENTED SINS

Confession, repentance and forgiveness will bring about such a release in your life that you would never want to be bound again.

This is a promise from God if we confess our sins. **1ˢᵗ John 1:9 declares,** *"If we confess our sins, He is faithful and just to forgive us our sins, and to cleanse us from all unrighteousness."*

Confession is telling the truth about you the majority of time.

Psalm 15: 1, 2 declares, *"Lord, who shall abide in thy tabernacle? Who shall dwell in thy holy hill? He that walketh uprightly, and worketh righteousness, and speaketh the truth in his heart."*

Now with all love, come out of somebody else's heart and speak the truth in your own heart.

Adam and Eve's confession to God was for their sake; for He knew that they had sinned against Him. **Genesis 3:8-13.**

Our confession is for our sakes, but it is easier to say *"it was him, it was her, and it was them."* Now we see where the inheritance of the spirit of blame comes from.

Why does God command us to confess?

1) Because He knows that we sin and we know that we sin, but He cannot activate forgiveness and cleansing until we confess.

2) When we confess, we are released from the bondage of sin that has a grip on our hearts and minds. Sin has claws and it won't let us go until we make up in our minds to do something about it and here is how we confess:

- We confess to God when we sin against Him. **Psalm 51:3, and 4a,** declares *"For I acknowledge my transgressions: and my sin is ever before me. Against thee, thee only, have I sinned and done this evil in thy sight."*

- We confess to our sins when the offense is against another person.

Matthew 5:23 declares, *"Therefore if thou bring thy gift to the altar, and there remeberest that thy brother hath aught against thee, leave there thy gift before the altar, and go thy way; first be reconciled to thy brother, and then come and offer thy gift."*

Offense stays in the Body of Christ because we have learned how to reason with ourselves against the Truth.

When we come before God to offer a sacrifice of praise, worship, ourselves, etc. and the <u>Holy Spirit</u> have been reminding us about a brother or sister that is offended with us, He doesn't accept our gift until we repent to all parties involved.

That is why there has been a breach in relationships in the Body of Christ and the fruit of our disobedience is the growing amount of broken relationships that God had to heal over the past years.

- **James 5:16a declares,** *"Confess your faults one to another, and pray one for another, that ye may be healed."* Confess your faults one to another is when God has divinely blessed you with someone who loves you unconditionally that you can trust to tell the truth about the real you. This scripture has the benefits of blessings, healing and deliverance in it. Every now and then, it is good to have a good old fashion sit down with someone you can trust and say, **"look, it is like this."**

One last note on confession: use wisdom when sharing your issues with someone because some people can't handle your pain.

Repentance means to **change** and **never return** to the sin anymore.

Repentance is not just saying "I am sorry", for God wants heart wrenching sorrow for the sin that was committed and complete turning away from it.

David when he had sinned against God with Bathsheba in the book of **2nd Samuel** was very sorrowful for his transgression against God. His prayer of confession and repentance in **Psalm 51** gives us an example on how God wants true confession and repentance. **Psalm 51:1-19**

Once he repented, David never returned to repeat that again.

Repentance means a change of mind that result in a change of conduct. It involves a complete change of attitude and behavior regarding the sin committed. It is by God's grace and mercy that leads us to repentance. **2nd Corinthians 7:10**

Jesus declares in **Matthew 3:8** *"Bring forth therefore fruits meet for repentance."*

Without the results of your repentance, it is hard to believe what we say and it seems like we are liars, especially when our behavior and conduct has not changed.

Pride and assumption is why many don't repent over their sins. **Ecclesiastes 8:11** *states, "Because sentence against an evil work is not executed speedily, therefore the heart of the sons of men is fully set in them to do evil."*

It is saying because the penalty of judgment is delayed because of God's longsuffering, man will assume they have gotten away with something and let their hearts continue to operate in evil.

God is requiring that we be obedient in confession and repentance and in that He will have mercy upon us.

5

<u>IRREVERENCE FOR THE HOUSE OF GOD</u>

Psalm 89:7 declares, *"God is greatly to be feared in the assembly of the saints, and to be had in reverence of all them that is about Him."*

The word *"greatly"* used in this context means abundant. Abundant in the Hebrew and Greek according to using it in the right context of the scriptures means **increase, exceedingly and more frequent.**

God is to be feared at all times with great fervency.

The mistakes we can make are *"in the assembly of the saints"* and think it is the only time for God to be reverenced, but the scripture also states, *"to be had in reverence of all them that are about Him."*

God is looking at us all the time and we are accountable on how we conduct ourselves before Him, even while we are not in church.

Reverence in this context means **to fear, to revere, to frighten, be (make) afraid, and to put in fear.**

God is a loving Father and it is Satan's will to plant a twisted seed of fear about God in our minds. He wants God's creation to believe that He is some hard, mean, brutish being sitting in heaven waiting to kill anyone who makes a mistake.

Fearing God is when one believes in Him and is not willfully sinning against Him.

It also means to have a great, deep and humble respect, realizing that we are nothing and He is everything.

Ecclesiastes 5:1 declares, *"Keep thy foot when thou goest to the house of God, and be more ready to hear, than to give the sacrifice of fools: for they consider not that they do evil."*

When we come into the house of God and the Spirit of the Lord is present, holding conversations that is not pertaining to praising and worshipping Him is disrespectful to Him in His house, **His house**.

We have to *"keep our feet",* by being mindful of ourselves on how we are carrying ourselves in reverencing God when we are in the sanctuary.

"Be ready to hear, than to give the sacrifice of fools." How are we going to hear what the Spirit of the Lord is saying, if we are talking when the Spirit of the Lord is talking?

Some of us hold whole conversations when He is speaking through a vessel because we don't understand His presence.

"For they consider not that they do evil" Why does God consider it evil?

Because the Holy Spirit is about to work the will of God and His Presence is not even being acknowledged and He considers it evil!

Evil in this context of scripture means, **displeasure, ill-favored, grief, hurt and sorrow.**

He is displeased because it is His will to come and dwell in the midst of us and release blessings upon His people.

Psalm 115:12, 13 declares, *"The Lord hath been mindful of us: He will bless us; He will bless the house of Israel; He will bless the house of Aaron. He will bless them that fear the Lord, both small and great."*

He wants to bless us when we are in His presence, but the key is having the fear of the Lord in our lives and our spiritual temple requires that same fear.

1st Corinthians 6:15, 19, 20 declares, *"Know ye not that your bodies are the members of Christ? shall I then take the members of Christ, and make them the members of a harlot? God forbid.*

What know? ye not that your body is the temple of the Holy Ghost which is in you, which ye have of God, and ye are not your own?

For ye are bought with a price: therefore glorify God in your body, and in your spirit, which are God's."

Our bodies are **members** of Christ. That means that we are an intricate part of Him and so attached to Him, that whatever we do, we do it to Him. Wow! What a revelation!

We need to **receive** this knowledge that God is dwelling on the inside of us. The scripture above says, **"What",** in other words, **"don't you know?"** Do you not have the understanding that God is living on the inside of you? Did you not know that the Holy Spirit is God?

Did you not know when we accepted Christ, who shedded His blood for us, bought us by paying the price for our salvation (**deliverance, safety, peace, prosperity, health and well-being**) and when we said yes to Him, we became solely His, being under His Authority, telling us what to do? The totality of us belongs to God, Spirit, Soul and Body.

Our bodies were created to glorify God, not only in praise and worship, but also in diet, exercise, rest and balance.

God doesn't receive any glory out of His people when our health is affected because we are not receiving enough rest and always on the go! That is one of the reasons why some of us cannot hear God's voice! How would you know when He is talking to you when you are sometimes spiritually incoherent?

One of the major epidemics in America is our dietary mindsets and it has become an epidemic in the Body of Christ.

Not only will it stop us from finishing purpose, but also it can cause premature death.

What is going on in the economy is hitting across the board and the effect of it is making people turn to find comfort even if it is food, drugs, alcohol and/or sex. But God intends for His people to be a beacon of light for the unbelievers to see the True and Living God so they can turn to Him and know that regardless, He is the answer to all their needs.

We must represent Him in spirit, soul and body that they may have hope and believe that when they look at us, they can be helped also.

Before I end this chapter, why did not I say anything about sin? Because if we are being taught the Word of God without compromise, we are not ignorant on how God looks at sin. But I found out even in that, we can ignore God and act like we don't know.

However, just in case you are not being taught in that measure, sin is:

- A breaking of God law (His Word) willingly and ignorantly.

Because some churches have not taught the Word of God in Truth and Righteousness, most people think sin is a part of a lifestyle to be excused and not to be delivered from!

When Jesus Christ died for us, He died for the totality of us spirit, soul and body. Nevertheless, if Truth and Righteousness regarding the Word of God is not being taught properly, it will leave an individual to believe that God is excusing their sin, but in reality we will answer to God on judgment day and for many who have not repented will find themselves in hell forever. **Romans 14:10**

God wants both of the temples to be reverenced because His presence being in both and we have a mandate from God for Him to be glorified *in* where we worship as well as *from* where we worship and that is in our bodies.

6

DISHONORING GOD'S LEADERSHIP AND AUTHORITY

This is the most deceptive of all spiritual toxins in the Body of Christ because of not understanding God regarding scripture.

If the generals from the past could be interviewed and even our current leaders they will tell you leading God's people is not peaches and cream. It really is not all that easy and some if they would be honest, they had thought about quitting and some did.

I write this humbly and I experienced being over a flock to a certain degree. Being a minister gives me some insight and let me taste being before people, but we are talking about those who God had assigned over a flock and didn't haven't a clue that when they were playing with trucks and dolls that one day, their life was going to be changed forever.

Because we and I say we, don't have a clue of the mandates, accountabilities and responsibilities that God Himself may place on them, we often think their job shouldn't be that challenging, but it is.

All of us will stand before God and give an account to our lives, but their positions not only have a greater accountability and responsibility, but a stricter judgment. *Romans 14:12, James 3:1*

We are going to look at two men I believe God is going to use for this chapter and that would be Moses and Jesus. They were sent, assigned and ordained by God to lead souls out of bondage.

Mosheh (original Hebrew) or *Moses*, a Hebrew son of slaves, put into the Nile River from Pharaoh's fear and paranoia of the Hebrews multiplying in population was drawn from the water by Pharaoh's daughter, nursed by his own mother, sent back to Pharaoh's daughter to become her son and rose up in Egypt to be become a great leader and warrior. He escaped slavery and lived a life that the rich and famous cannot even imagine or touch. Let us look some of his life:

- **Trained in the Egyptian court in "the wisdom of the Egyptians."**
- **Learned the mysteries of the Egyptian religion, arithmetic, geometry, poetry, music, medicine, and hieroglyphics.**
- **He was the general of the Egyptian armies.**
- **He lived in the columns of Egypt, known for its majesty of marble, stone and glory.**
- **Moses had the best education, training and skills that I believe all of our colleges combined couldn't even touch.**

Moses was a Hebrew. Pharaoh knew it, his daughter knew it, his parents knew it, Moses knew it and even the Hebrew slaves knew it. **Exodus 2:1-10, Hebrew 11:23-24**

He was in a position of such greatness and authority because of God's plan. But when Moses fled from Pharaoh for killing an Egyptian, he ran into the One who really had His eye on him and that was God. **Exodus 3:1-4**

Moses was forty years old when God called for him and eighty years old when God sent him out.

God first introduced Himself and gave Moses forty years of direction and training him on who God is and then took all of his training, skill, wisdom and education that he learned from Egypt to use for His Glory.

He did not need anything from Moses and the same thing applies to us today. But He chooses vessels to lead His flock.

It was over two million people that God used Moses to lead out of Egypt. Two people with different personalities can be something else, but over two million?

You had the rebellious, the uncommitted and the opinionated crowd. The *"I don't believe God"* crowd, the **"attitude"** crowd, the *"I don't feel like it"* crowd, the *"why do we have to do this way"* crowd, *"Moses is not God"* crowd, *"God is not God"* crowd, *"If I can't have it my way, I will go back to Egypt"* crowd, okay you get the picture and if we would be honest, some of us were once a part of this crowd and still are!

Now, mind you there were some of them who made his life easy, but for the most part, the children of Israel gave Moses the blues before they left Egypt even up to his death. Their stubbornness and rebellion caused Moses to lose his temper and disobey God's command and God judged him and he was not allowed to cross over into the promise land. **Numbers 20:10-12**

But for the most part Moses went into intercession for them because of their complaints which were offensive to God and Moses having a relationship with God knew that God did not care for their ways and God was about to kill them!

Even though Moses was God's set man, he also needed to be refreshed and energized in dealing with the children of Israel. He stayed in God's presence because he knew in that in the natural he could not lead them. He also knew in the natural they deserved their judgment because of their stubbornness and rebellion, but if he stayed in God's presence, he could intercede for them and continue with God's vision and receive His grace.

The set man and/or woman of God that has been placed over us can attest to that some of us are a piece of work and it has been prayer and intercession that has kept God's mercy and grace activated in our lives, can I get a witness? Thank you sister!

These leaders of God do not choose their lives, God does! Nobody in their right mind wants to deal with over two million different personalities and dispositions, let alone under five hundred to thousands! Nevertheless, when God calls you for the task, **He Himself** has already equipped and empowered you for the call and with Him you find out all things are possible, even leading a flock.

Which brings us to Korah and he kept me puzzled about his actions.

Korah was a Levite and they were separated to come near to God to serve in the tabernacle worship and to stand before the congregation to minister.

Numbers 16:9

As a minister that task calls for accountability and responsibility before God especially when there are requirements and mandates.

Korah wanted a greater position of authority than he already had. He wanted to be able to stand before people and be recognized as **"the Authority."**   In the book of Numbers the 16th chapter, we have Korah, Dathan, and Abiram and with 250 princes the Bible states they were **"famous in the congregation, men of renown."** These men were honored and held weight with the people.

This is a piece of wisdom I must share: Leaders, if your influence carries weight with the people, but you are not the set man or woman of the house, humble yourself and always point the people to the Truth and Righteousness of God and don't do anything that would cause an uproar inside the house because people may favor you greatly.

We are not dealing with you, but with God's Kingdom.

They accused Moses of *"taking too much upon himself"*. Now seriously, did they even take a look at all those people he was dealing with? Their problems and issues and having to be judge at the same time? No, because when you want a place of *"unauthorized authority"* you can't see because of your pride, thinking that you can handle the position better!

Look at the position God had set the Levites in:

- **To separate them from Israel.**
- **To bring them near to Himself to serve in the tabernacle to worship.**
- **To stand before the congregation to minister to them.**

The children of Israel couldn't get that close to God! Just to be chosen to come near Him was an honor let alone to be in His Presence and serve Him!

It should have been a humbling experience to stand before people who knows that you are flesh like them and you have to sacrifice for your own sins and be a mouth piece for God!

But Moses revealed the truth of the whole matter in **Numbers 16:9-11 and it declares, *"Seemeth it but a small thing unto you, that the God of Israel hath separated you from the congregation of Israel, to bring you near to himself to do the service of the tabernacle of the Lord, and to stand before the congregation to minister unto them?***

And he hath brought thee near to him, and all they brethren the sons of Levi with thee: and seek ye the priesthood also?

For which cause both thou and all thy company are gathered together against the Lord: and what is Aaron that you murmur against him?

Why did Korah trip with Aaron? What did he want? He was already in position as a priest, but he wanted the *"office"* of the priesthood, which belonged to Aaron at that present time.

If you seeking to be in leadership, ask yourself why do I really want to be in leadership? If you are in leadership, ask yourself, why you really want to be in leadership. Sounds redundant, but it is the truth.

Every year I take myself before God and ask Him what is my real motives of being a leader. Am I serving because He placed me or have I gone astray and want to stay in position for security and title purposes?

Did Moses pray and intercede for them? No, because this offense was not done out of ignorance.

The children of Israel offended God many times at the beginning and God was merciful because He knew their messed up mindsets along with their hardened hearts. If He could by showing them His strength and power change their minds, it would have changed their hearts.

Nevertheless, about the time they have gotten to the point of their journey, God was holding them accountable because not only did they see, but experienced God's works and had a general idea that they needed to line up.

Judgment was sent because of their rebellion, not ignorance, and Korah, Dathan, Abiram not only died, but the 250 princes with their families and 14,700 people along with them according to **Numbers 16:49** and these are the offenses:

- **Rebellion**
- **Disrespect to God**
- **Disrespect to God's Set Man**
- **Dishonoring their Position**

- **No Humbleness**
- **No Repentance**
- **Bringing Confusion in the Camp**
- **Causing Judgment**

We all have crossed that line with God and His grace and mercy is keeping us from judgment, but I would not willfully try God in this area because His judgments still stand and His Word doesn't change, neither what He has set in order. He only can change order.

Their actions caused not only death to themselves, but their families and brought murmuring and complaining from the children of Israel and caused God to judge them also. **Numbers 16:23-27, Numbers 16:41- 49.**

HaMashiach Yeshua – Jesus Christ

Jesus (Hebrew-Yeshua) means *"Savior" or "God, Who is Salvation."*

Jesus Christ was, still and will always be the most controversial Leader of all times.

The saddest thing to find out when this life is over is that Jesus is real and He is the **only** most important thing we ever needed while we were living on this earth.

His mission is a spiritual one and Satan wants to disannul who He is, *__Jesus Christ the Son of the Living God__*.

Adam's act of disobedience to God's command was the worst human tragedy that ever happened on earth. The fall of mankind was more detrimental to the human race than can ever be described.

Even though Eve was present, God held Adam more accountable because the command came to him first. **1st Timothy 2:13-14** declares

"And Adam was first formed, then Eve. And Adam was not deceived, but the woman being deceived was in the transgression."

Adam was well aware of God's commandment. Satan deceived Eve, she fell into sin and influenced Adam into joining her and both had caused something catastrophic that affects the whole human race until this day. It is called sin.

Sin, what is sin? **It is a violation or shall I say a breaking of God's laws, commandments and statues**.

 Who have sinned? **Romans 3:23** declares all have, *"For all have sinned, and come short of the glory of God."*

 To break things down, we are spiritual beings created in the image of God. **Genesis 1:26a** declares, *"And God said, Let us make man in our image, after our likeness."*

God created man in His image, in His Spirit and His likeness.

The dictionary meaning of image is *a reproduction or imitation of, exact likeness* and I love this one*, a striking resemblance and semblance, meaning actual or apparent resemblance*. Wow! That is how God created us before sin entered in our lives!

 What is the image of God?

- God is Holy. **Leviticus 19:2b "Ye shall be holy: for I am the Lord your God is holy."**   Man was created in holiness.

- God is righteous. **Psalm 145:17 "The Lord is righteous in all His ways and holy in all His works."**   Man was created in righteousness.

- Here is one that we never think about: the Fruit of the Spirit, which is God's Spirit. This is God's image and man was created in that also. **Galatians 5:22 declares, "But the fruit of the Spirit is**

love, joy, peace, longsuffering, gentleness, goodness, faith, meekness, temperance: against such there is no law."

This is the will of God for the whole human race!

Well, who brought the sin? Who else? I know some of you might want to think the woman did, but she didn't. There is an archenemy on earth and his name is Satan.

He rebelled against God with two-thirds of the Angels and they all got booted out of heaven. **Revelations 12:9, 12**

He is the **originator of sin** and his plan is to get back at God anyway he can, especially when he saw us (male and female) being created in the image of God.

He went after Eve and deceived her by twisting the words God commanded and through her act of curiosity and disobedience, she gave Satan the opportunity to transfer his spirit into her heart and she became his image, which is the opposite of the list above.

Now someone brought a point to me and asked the question. Why Adam did not notice the change in Eve? What did she do that made her seem like the same person he just saw minutes ago?

Now this is my take, deception is a spirit that doesn't want to be exposed. A deceiving spirit wants to hide the truth in order for the false to prevail, but it must be wrapped right with a little truth and must be mixed in it so the false won't be exposed.

The change that went on with Eve was on the inside of her because on the outside she still *looked the same* and *sounded like herself*!

That is enough to make you stay very prayerful! She influenced Adam to disobey God and in that both became one in the same sin.

It affected the whole human race and everyone born on the face of the earth is imaged in sin. **Romans 5:11, 14** states, *"Wherefore, as by one man sin entered into the world, and death by sin; and so death passed upon all men, for that all have sinned:*

14 Nevertheless deaths reigned from Adam to Moses, even over them that had not sinned after the similitude of Adam's transgression, who is the figure of him that was to come."

Now, before you declare that it isn't fair and you had nothing to do with it, it was passed down to us by default and regardless of your take on it, it is true. The bottom line is we were sinners from birth.

Well, does sin have a look? Sure it does, but it starts from our heart (which is not always detected) and then manifests itself through the flesh (actions, behavior, conduct). Although we put a suit, dress and perfume on ourselves the manifestation of what is in us do come out.

Mark 7:21-23 declares *"For from within out of the heart of men, proceed evil thoughts, adulteries, fornications, murders, 22 Thefts, covetousness, wickedness, deceit, lasciviousness, an evil eye, blasphemy, pride, foolishness: 25 All these evil things come from within and defile the man."*

That is some of the list and to not be deceived, there are little foxes that one can do, that we have learned how to operate in and think it is okay. Now, we all can see a little more clearly!

Sin transitioned into Adam and Eve's heart through their disobedience and we became a by-product of their environment and God knew one thing; we were going to need a Savior.

The controversy that surrounds Jesus Christ was His mission down here on earth.

He came to save man's soul from three things, God's judgment, Eternal Death and the Lake of Fire.

Some don't believe they will live eternally somewhere when they die, but we will, either with Christ or eternal damnation in the lake of fire with Satan and his angels.

God knew that because of sin, He would have to judge someone and we were top pick, but His love is so deep and rich that He could not see us receiving what we deserved so He sent someone who was ***willing*** and ***very capable*** in taking our place and His name is **Jesus**. **Romans 5:8 declares** *"But God commendeth His love toward us, in that, while we ye sinners, Christ died for us."*

This is the mission of Christ and it being a spiritual one has to be received by faith.

The controversy regarding Jesus is that human nature wants to see, feel and touch before we believe. We want evidence before we can say it is valid. We are still trying to find something that says Jesus is real.

If we can put it in our finite minds and say okay, here it is, what I am discovering is valid, and then we ***might*** believe.

The spirit of deception that Satan used against Eve is still working and he wants to do everything within his power for no one to believe gospel of Jesus Christ.

1ˢᵗ Corinthians 4:3, 4 declares, *"But if our gospel be hid, it is hid to them that are lost: In whom the god of this world hath blinded the minds of them which believe not, lest the light of the glorious gospel of Christ, who is the image of God, should shine unto them."*

Here we have examples of two great leaders, not to put them both in the same category of purpose, mission, stature or greatness because Christ is greater than all, but for us to see how God is trying to lead people out of captivity and will use men and women for the task.

When He chooses them, He has also approved them and He also knows what He has ordered.

Antidote

What is an antidote? A remedy for an illness and this poison that has crept up in the church needs one and it is called repentance and submission to God's Word.

We all have been guilty and found ourselves in one or many of the categories listed.

But when God dealt with me about these things I saw the subtlety of Satan to have us focus on the outward things only and not check our hearts.

If He is dealing with your heart about these poisons, allow Him to minister to you so you won't be infiltrated and you find yourself becoming defiled without even knowing it.

God wants to bless His people, but until we not only learn the will of God, but also do the will of God, we won't experience the glorious blessings He has for us.

If you find that you have been infiltrated with any of these toxins, acknowledge it before God and allow Him to cleanse you and whatever He leads you to do follow Him so you can be free.

God bless,
Minister Joyce A. Nash

*If you are not saved, you can accept Christ as your personal Savior today. It is never too late to give your heart to Christ.

Bibliography

Dake, Finis. *Dake's Annotated Reference Bible: The Holy Bible, Containing the Old and New Testaments of the Authorized or King James Version Text ... and a Complete Concordance and Cyclopedic Index.* Atlanta, GA: Dake Bible Sales, 1963. Print.

King James Bible. Nashville, TN: Holman Bible, 1973. Print.

Parsons, John J. "Hebrew Names for God." *Www.hebrews4christians.com.* Hebrew for Christians, n.d. Web. 14 Nov. 2015.

Strong, James. *The Exhaustive Concordance of the Bible: Showing Every Word of the Text of the Common English Version of the Canonical Books, and Every Occurrence of Each Word in Regular Order, Together with a Key-word Comparison of Selected Words and Phrases in the King James Version with Five Leading Contemporary Translations, Also Brief Dictionaries of the Hebrew and Greek Words of the Original, with References to the English Words.* Nashville: Abingdon, 1980. Print.

About the Author

 God called me into ministry in 1991 with the anointing to teach and preach the Word, laying a good foundation in me through prayer and the Word of God. He ordained me in 2001 as a minister of the gospel by his choosing and direction.

God trained me under many excellent pastors and ministries, especially through the school of prayer called "Show Me Myself." This school through the Holy Spirit trains a person to become humble, compassionate and merciful to the next person.

Hadassah Ministries was founded in 1999 with a vision to strengthen and empower men and women through the power of God's Word. Our mission is for souls to be restored and prosper in all five areas: physically, spiritually, naturally, emotionally and financially.

In 2009, God directed me to go out and evangelize, conducting women seminars and teaching according to God's will.

Hadassah Ministries has a blog, *Hadassah2012.blogspot.com. FB: Hadassah Ministries* and/or *Minister Joyce A. Nash*, along with several newsletters such as *"Notable"* and *"Girl, I Need a Word."*

I am a mother of two children both called to fulfill destiny.

Hadassah Ministries is registered with the State of Missouri. All publication is under Hadassah Ministries. ©2016 All rights reserved.

Made in the USA
Monee, IL
28 October 2021